P9-DOE-983

DIVING AND SNORKELING GUIDE TO

The
BritishVirgin Islands

Linda Sorensen

Pisces Books
A division of Gulf Publishing Company
Houston, Texas

Publisher's note: At the time of publication of this book, all the information was determined to be as accurate as possible. However, when you use this guide, new construction may have changed land reference points, weather may have altered reef configurations, and some businesses may no longer be in operation. Your assistance in keeping future editions up-to-date will be greatly appreciated.

Also, please pay particular attention to the diver rating system in this book. Know your limits!

This guide was reviewed by author
and reprinted August 1995.

Copyright © 1992 by Gulf Publishing Company, Houston, Texas. All rights reserved. This book, or parts thereof, may not be reproduced in any form without permission of the publisher.
All photographs are by the authors.

 **Pisces Books®**
A division of Gulf Publishing Company
P.O. Box 2608
Houston, Texas 77525-2608

Pisces Books is a registered trademark of Gulf Publishing Company.
Printed in Hong Kong

10   9   8   7   6   5   4   3

Library of Congress Cataloging-in-Publication Data

Sorensen, Linda
    Diving and snorkeling guide to the British Virgin Islands /
Linda Sorensen.
        p.   cm.
    Includes index.
    ISBN 1-55992-050-5
    1. Skin diving—British Virgin Islands—Guide-books.
2. Scuba diving—British Virgin Islands—Guide-books.
3. British Virgin Islands—Description and travel/1981—
Guide-books   I. Title.
GV840.S78S62   1991
797.2′3′09729725—dc20   91-689
                                                         CIP

Table of Contents

How To Use This Guide

This guide was developed to familiarize you with the location and topography of a variety of dive sites in the British Virgin Islands. Most readers will be diving with a shore-based dive operation or from a live-aboard dive boat, so you will not be required to find the sites yourself and will be shown the highlights of the dive underwater. But, when the planned dive is announced, you will have a good idea of what to expect in terms of depth, current, topography, and photo subjects. For those who are diving on their own, this guide will help you choose your sites and point out important safety considerations.

The Rating System for Divers and Dives

To be safe, this guide is conservative regarding the minimum level of expertise required for any given dive, citing the old adage about there being old divers and bold divers but few old bold divers. A novice diver is someone in decent physical condition who has recently completed a basic certification diving course, or a certified diver who has not been diving recently or who has no experience in similar waters. An intermediate diver is a certified diver in excellent physical condition who has been diving actively for at least a year following a basic course, and who has been diving recently in similar waters. An advanced diver is someone who has completed an advanced certification diving course, has been diving recently in similar waters, and is in excellent physical condition. You will have to decide if you are capable of making any particular dive, depending on your level of training, as well as water conditions at the site. Remember that water conditions can change at any time, even during a dive.

The dives are listed under the island to which they are closest, working up the Sir Francis Drake Channel from west to east. Tortola- based dive companies most frequently dive the sites near Norman, Peter, Salt, Cooper and Ginger. Virgin Gorda-based dive companies dive the sites near Salt, Cooper, Ginger, The Dogs, Virgin Gorda, and Anegada. Live-aboard charter boats spend their week moving from island to island, so at any time are close to number of good sites.

There are many dives that are tricky to locate, and these are best visited with an experienced local guide. I have indicated this in the text. Two sites, the Caves at Norman Island, and the Baths at Virgin Gorda are best enjoyed by snorkeling and are listed here because they are highlights of any trip to the BVI.

◀ *Welcome to the British Virgin Islands! (Photo: Jim Scheiner.)*

1

Overview of the British Virgin Islands

History

The British Virgin Islands are a string of more than 40 islands, rocks, and cays scattered on each side of the Sir Francis Drake Channel, 60 miles east of Puerto Rico, and 1,100 miles southeast of Miami. With steady tradewinds, well protected anchorages, and a year-round balmy climate, the BVI is an idyllic cruising area that attracts thousands of divers and sailors each year.

Oceanic in origin, the British Virgin Islands emerged from the seabed by the uplifting and folding of submerged volcanoes 70-100 million years ago. As recently as the last ice age, 15,000 years ago, when the sea level was 300 feet lower, these islands were connected by land to Puerto Rico and the U.S. Virgin Islands. Today they stand as peaks of a drowned mountain range.

The Virgin Islands are located at the apex of a sweeping chain of islands that extend from Trinidad to Florida. A natural stopping point for boats traveling a tradewind route, this location has been a prime influence in the history of the islands from the first Ciboney Indians that arrived in their Stone Age canoes to the ships sailing the trade routes between Europe and the Americas.

Following the Ciboney Indians, Arawak Indians arrived about 100 BC, migrating from the Orinoco Basin in South America. A peaceloving tribe, they settled throughout the Caribbean, cultivating the land and making pottery, some of which can still be found today.

◄
Elkhorn coral and colorful reef fish such as this rock beauty are often seen snorkeling or diving in the British Virgin Islands. (Photo: Jim Scheiner.)

3

Verdant green slopes of the north side of Tortola drop to long stretches of isolated white beaches. (Photo: Jim Scheiner.)

About a hundred years before the arrival of Columbus, the aggressive and warlike Carib Indians arrived from South America in huge dugout canoes. They moved throughout the Caribbean, terrorizing the Arawak settlements, stealing the women, and taking the young boys to be fattened and eaten. The Caribs drove the Arawaks north where they eventually became extinct under Spanish slavery.

Columbus discovered the Virgin Islands in 1493 on his second trip to the New World. Seeing so many small islands surrounding larger ones, he names them "Las Once Mil Virgines" in honor of St. Ursula and her

11,000 virgin followers. He also gave Virgin Gorda (the fat virgin) and Anegada (the sunken island) the names that remain today.

As the Spanish settled throughout the West Indies, the Caribs continued their aggressive ways towards the Spanish and their galleons carrying riches from South and Central America to Spain. Other forms of piracy and privateering also developed, supported by Europeans who were afraid to challenge the Spanish directly. An assortment of colorful characters and explorers sailed through the waters of the Virgin Islands: pirates Henry Morgan, Sir John Hawkins, and the fearless Blackbeard, and explorers Ponce de Leon and Sir Francis Drake, after whom the main channel is named.

As other countries began to colonize and the power of Spain diminished, the islands went through a long period of shifting ownership. Eventually, the Danes took possession of St. Thomas, and the English ousted the Dutch from Tortola and Virgin Gorda. With the introduction of sugarcane production in the 1640s and the practice of slavery, a plantation economy was gradually established. At first, Tortola was occupied by planters who were more interested in piracy and smuggling than agriculture, but by the 1700s they were displaced by more serious planters. From the 1750s

Looking through the cut between Green Cay and Little Jost Van Dyke, with Sandy Cay in the background. Green Cay and Sandy Cay are popular day-sail destinations. (Photo: Jim Scheiner.)

This man on a donkey herding cattle represents a part of the old way of life on Tortola that coexists with the modern. (Photo: Jim Scheiner.)

to the 1850s, the islands prospered, producing sugar, cotton, rum, indigo, and spices.

As the number of slaves on the plantations grew, so did the severity of the punishment to control them, and controversy over the practice of slavery grew. With the ravages of several hurricanes and droughts, and a revival of fighting and piracy within the islands due to the American Revolution and Napoleonic wars, slaves suffered even more. By the mid-1800s slave rebellions resulted in their freedom. This, coupled with the introduction of the sugar beet into Europe, was disastrous for the "Trade Triangle" based on the production of sugar cane. The islands went into a decline as capital and people left the islands, and for the next 100 years the island economy was marginal.

In 1917, the United States purchased the Danish Virgin Islands to have a military outpost in the Caribbean. Progress continued to be slow in the British Virgin Islands, but gradual economic growth and social reform moved the islands towards local government. In the 1930s and '40s live-stock, vegetables, and fishing were still the mainstay of the economy. But by the '60s, Laurance Rockefeller leased land in Virgin Gorda and built the first luxury resort at Little Dix Bay. The airport at Beef Island was opened in 1968 and the opening of "The Moorings" in 1969 marked the beginning of the yachting industry in the BVI. In 1967, a ministerial system of government was introduced and BVIslanders were given the right to administer their own affairs.

Today, the economic and political stability of the BVI coupled with an ideal climate and unspoiled natural environment attract many visitors. Fortunately, local citizens are taking steps to guide the growth in the BVI, learning from the mistakes of other islands to protect the natural resources elemental to the tourist economy.

The Islands

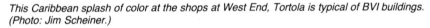

These volcanic islands, with green mountain peaks rising from aquamarine waters, vary in rainfall, sun, and wind exposure and therefore in vegetation. Hibiscus, bouganvilla, and mango thrive in moist areas; mangroves, seagrapes, and palms line the seashores; and cactus, fangipani, and wild tamarind cling to arid hillsides.

Tortola. This is the largest of the islands, 12 miles long and 3 miles wide. Dominated by a ridge of mountain peaks covered in green, the

This Caribbean splash of color at the shops at West End, Tortola is typical of BVI buildings. (Photo: Jim Scheiner.)

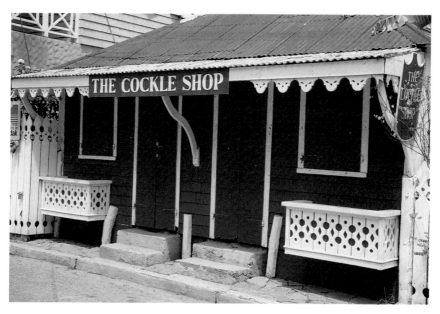

Small shops line the winding main street of Roadtown, Tortola. (Photo: Linda Sorensen.)

hills on the north side drop to sandy white beaches fringed with groves of palm trees. Mount Sage is the highest point on the island at 1,740 feet. A shady trail winds through a luxuriant rain forest. The north side catches and retains more rainfall, so mangoes, bananas, almonds, and breadfuit grow easily. The north side has the feel of old Tortola, with a pastoral, unstructured ambiance. An older Tortolan woman tends her sweet potatoes on the steep hillside; a gnarled fisherman repairs his nets under the shade of an almond tree; his neighbor loads a charcoal pit with green wood. Cows and goats graze on the hillside and the crow of the rooster greets each new day.

Tortola has a population of over 9,000, a large percentage of the BVI's approximately 12,000 total. Commerical activity centers around Road-town, the capital of the BVI. Several marinas line the waterfront of Road Harbour, home to a large charter fleet. Colorfully painted shops, open air restaurants, several pubs, and many banks and administrative buildings reveal a working West Indian town with a British influence.

Beef Island. Named after the cattle the buccaneers left to roam and later hunt, Beef Island is now the site of a 3,600-foot airstrip that serves as the primary airport for the BVI. The island is conveniently connected to Tortola by the small Queen Elizabeth drawbridge. A five-minute walk from the airport is the excellent anchorage of Trellis Bay, convenient for the yachtsmen.

Virgin Gorda. With a population of about 1,400 on 15 square miles of area, this island is a popular vacation destination with a variety of hotels, an unhurried attitude, and interesting topography. The northern half of the island is mountainous, dominated by Gorda Peak, which reaches 1,380 feet. North Sound, a large protected bay encircled by reef and islands, is a favorite anchorage for yachtsman and home to several resorts. The southern half of the island is flat and dry and noted for the giant granite boulders strewn across white beaches. "The Baths," one of the main attractions of the BVI, is a delightful playground of secret rooms, pools, and caves created by these huge boulders. With 20 beaches on Virgin Gorda, those near the Baths are the most visited. An abandoned Copper Mine on the southeast end of the island is a reminder of days past.

The scent of freshly baked breads tempt the visitor strolling through Roadtown. (Photo: Linda Sorensen.)

Chartering a boat is a good way to maximize your time on and under the waters of the BVIs. (Photo: Jim Scheiner.)

Anegada. Unique to the Virgin Islands, Anegada is a flat coral and limestone island. Its highest point is only 28 feet above sea level and miles of isolated white beaches line the northern and western shores. A reef extends 10 miles to the southeast of Anegada, the site of hundreds of ship wrecks over the years, creating unlimited exploration grounds for the diver. There are about 200 people on the island, a 2,500-foot airstrip, and one hotel. Anegada is a place for people who enjoy a sense of remoteness, and the feeling of nothing but sea and reef for miles around.

Across the Sir Francis Drake Channel from Roadtown lie a string of islands that provide excellent dive sites. **Cooper Island** has a few homes, a beach bar and a boat jetty, **Peter Island** has lovely beaches and a luxury resort, and **Salt Island** is famed as the site of the wreck of the *Rhone*. **Fallen Jerusalem**, **Round Rock**, **Ginger**, **Dead Chest**, and **Norman Island** are uninhabited. Conveniently located within a half-hour boat ride from Tortola, the sites are ideal for divers staying on Tortola. Many of these islands have excellent achorages and provide an ideal situation for live aboard charter yachts.

Mountainous **Jost Van Dyke**, with a population of about 130, lies northwest of Tortola. A sleepy settlement by day, Jost has lovely beaches and several noted beach bar restaurants that capture the barefoot ambiance of uninhibited island life. This island is surrounded by several small island gems, such as **Little Jost Van Dyke**, **Green Cay**, and **Sandy Cay**, often used as day-sail destinations.

Guana, **Great Camanoe**, **Scrub**, **Marina Cay**, **George Dog**, **Great Dog**, **West Dog**, **Mosquito**, **Saba**, **Necker**, and **Eustatia**, lie off of the east end of Tortola and off Virgin Gorda. A few are the home of special island resorts that take no more than 30 guests, and most have excellent diving or snorkeling off their shores. Part of the joy of a trip to the BVI is discovering the variety of island hideaways, a pastime that may take many visits.

Where To Stay, Ashore and Afloat

Ashore, the visitor can choose from an array of charming small inns and guesthouses, casual to elegant hotel complexes, private rental homes,

Cuan Law *is a 105-foot live-aboard diving charter boat with 6 crew members that caters to 20 guests in 10 private cabins, here anchored at Dead Man's Bay, Peter Island between dives. (Photo: Jim Scheiner.)*

or even campgrounds. Most of the accommodations are available on Tortola and Virgin Gorda, but the islands of Jost Van Dyke, Peter, Cooper, Guana, Great Camanoe, Marina Cay, Necker, Beef, Mosquito, and Anegada also offer unique and intimate resorts or rental homes. It is not unusual to find as few as 10 to 20 other guests at these hideaways that emphasize friendliness and personal service.

For those who choose to explore the islands afloat, there are many boats available for charter, either with crew or without. Both have become popular options in the Virgin Islands in the last 30 years, with boats departing from Tortola, Virgin Gorda, or St. Thomas. A number of crewed charter boats are fully scuba equipped with divemaster or instructor aboard and make diving the primary focus of the week. Other boats emphasize sailing, snorkeling, and exploring with scuba an occasional activity.

On a crewed charter boat the captain and crew are your hosts and design a tailor made itinerary for you. They escort you through the islands, sharing local knowedge, guiding both shore and water excursions, and ensuring the safe navigation and anchoring of the boat. The food served is usually excellent and abundant. With the personal service and comfort typical of most charter boats, guests feel relaxed and at home. More than

Charter yachts have a wide selection of protected harbors to choose from and sail from one idyllic location to another within a few hours. (Photo: Jim Scheiner.)

Carnival is a highly anticipated event each August in Roadtown. Here a Mocho Jumbie on stilts towers above the other celebrants. She is one of several Jumbies that add to the carnival spirit. (Photo: Linda Sorensen.)

13

200 crewed charter boats, ranging in size from 30-250 feet sail through BVI waters.

If you choose to bareboat charter, you are the crew, making your own navigating and sailing decisions, preparing your own meals, or sampling the cuisine of the various restaurants ashore that cater to sailors.

Shore-based dive operators offer "rendezvous" diving to charter boats. They meet the sailors at their boat, take them diving, and return them to their own boat afterwards. This is a good way to accommodate diving and non-diving members of a cruising group and still use the knowledge and expertise of local guides.

Getting There

You can fly into San Juan, Puerto Rico, St. Thomas, or St. Croix and take a connecting flight to Beef Island or Virgin Gorda. Most hotels or boats can be reached by a short taxi trip from the airport. Because lost or delayed luggage is sometimes a problem, have a carry-on bag with essentials (or everything) with you, and be sure all bags are locked, especially scuba bags. Ferry services run between St. Thomas, St. John, Tortola, Virgin Gorda, Peter Island, Jost Van Dyke, and on some days, Anegada. For a price, there are also water taxi services available.

A current listing of ferry schedules, transportation services and BVI accommodations, ashore and afloat, can be found in the *Welcome* magazine, available from the BVI Tourist Board, P.O. Box 134, Road-town, Tortola. Phone: 809-494-3134; 800-835-8530.

Customs and Immigration

Visitors are welcome up to six months, if they possess return or ongoing tickets, evidence of adequate means of support and accommodations during their stay. A passport is the preferred requirement for entry, how-ever for U.S. and Canadian citizens a valid birth certificate or voter's registration card will suffice. Visitors from some countries may also need a visa. The BVI is very stict about the possession of illegal drugs, which constitutes a criminal offense. Jail and stiff fines can result from conviction and visitors are not immune to punishment.

Currency

The currency of the BVI is the US dollar. Major credit cards are accepted at most establishments.

2

Diving in the British Virgin Islands

The Virgin Islands are part of a huge underwater shelf that extends eastward about 85 miles from Puerto Rico to Anegada, then drops sharply into the Caribbean on the south and the Atlantic on the north. Because all of the sport diving is done on this shelf, most of the diving in the BVI is less than 70 feet. With over 40 rocks, cays, and islands, many underwater pinnacles, and several wrecks in a reasonable depth of water, the diving is remarkably diverse and interesting. The whole span of the islands lies within 35 miles, so most sites are within a 20- or 30-minute ride from Tortola or Virgin Gorda.

Diving is easy and convenient off the stable platform of a fully equipped live-aboard dive boat that anchors near the dive site. (Photo: Jim Scheiner.)

Diving in the BVI provides a tremendous variety of underwater topography — rock pinnacles that jut up from 60 feet to the surface; caverns created by giant underwater boulders; walls painted in colorful sponges; caves; ledges; overhangs; and fascinating wrecks provide home for an abundance of tropicals. There are more than 50 commonly known sites, and many more when the personal favorites of individual dive guides are included.

Diving in the BVI is year round. There is always a site that will have good conditions. Seasoned divers have discovered that there are advantages to the summer "off season" — the islands have fewer tourists, airfares and accommodation rates are lower, and the seas are calmer.

The land-based dive operations and live-aboard dive boats meet the professional standards that you would expect in the States. Guides are instructors, divemasters, or assistant instructors certified by the major training organizations. C-cards and sometimes logbooks are required by all operations. For nondivers most companies offer an introductory course that allows the student to dive the same day with the supervision of an instructor. Major brands of diving equipment are available for sale or rent and can be repaired locally. But it is a good idea to have your annual gear servicing at home before you leave.

Weather

The BVI has a balmy subtropical climate, ideal year round. Winter temperatures range from 75-85°F; summer temperatures range from 80-90°, both with about a 5-10° degree drop at night. The most noticeable difference however, is the wind speed, which ranges from 15 to 20 knots in winter, with occasional higher gusts, but is a more tranquil 10-15 knot breeze in the summer. The strenth of the wind affects the amount of chop at the exposed dive sites.

The average wave height in the winter is 3-5 feet at sea, with waves in the channel often less, due to the protection of the islands. When the wind subsides, the waters can be almost lakelike.

In the winter months an important factor to consider is the north swell: long slow waves from 5 to 10 feet high that come crashing onto the north side and make diving there untenable. The north swell is a result of storms in the North Atlantic, and may last for three days to a week or so, then subside. When the north swell is up, divemasters and captains choose from the abundance of protected sites on the south side of the islands. A day or so after the swells have stopped the water settles and the north side is again open for exploration.

There is rarely a north swell in the spring, summer, and fall, when the gentler winds allow for comfortable anchoring and calm boat trips. This

Winter swells roll onto the lovely beach at Long Bay, on the north side of Tortola, a result of storms in the North Atlantic. (Photo: Jim Scheiner.)

makes summer a favorite time for local and knowledgeable visiting divers, who set out to explore any site they choose, unhampered by the weather.

June to December is officially hurricane season, with the watch most vigilant late summer and fall. However, weather reporting is so good now that you'll have days of warning in advance of any approaching threat, so there's no reason to miss the chance for a good dive trip during this time.

Water temperatures at the surface range from 77-79°F in the winter and 78-80 °F in the summer. At depth, temperatures can drop several degrees so a wetsuit is often desirable for someone doing a lot of diving, especially in the winter.

Visibility

Visibility usually ranges from 60 to 130 feet, with the areas of greatest clarity around the smaller islands, rocky pinnacles, and offshore sea-mounts. With careful selection of dive sites, good visibility can usually be found any time of year.

Excellent visibility at offshore pinnacles allow divers to spot pelagics such as this spotted eagle ray. (Photo: Jim Scheiner.)

Currents

The tidal range is only about one foot so current is not a problem in protected areas. However, at some dive sites exposed to the open sea or in a channel between islands, currents can be strong. Obtain local information about the conditions of the site you choose, note the direction of the current before you go in, plan your dive accordingly, and ideally dive with support personnel in a boat on the surface.

Marine Protection and Conservation

One of the most valuable resources of the BVI is the natural environment and, fortunately, steps are being taken to protect the islands and the underwater world. There are several areas of conservation that visitors should know about.

Established in 1961 and initiated with a gift from Laurance Rockefeller, the BVI National Parks Trust manages the Territory's parks and protected areas and works to save endangered species such as the Anegada iguana, the humpback whale, the leatherback, hawksbill and green turtles, and nesting seabirds. Other Trust projects include the reforestation of Sage Mountain and Gorda Peak, establishment of the the Botanical Gardens in Roadtown and the development of an environmental education program for local schools. They are also stabilizing the historic Copper Mine on Virgin Gorda.

In the past few years, the National Parks Trust, in conjunction with the BVI Diver Operators Association, has instituted a mooring system to protect the reef from careless anchoring. Using funds raised through the Trust and the contributions of time and materials from various local dive businesses in the area, moorings have been placed at numerous dive sites and several popular snorkeling areas. When the plan is fully implemented there will be 200 moorings in place.

Yellow moorings are designated for commercial dive boat use only. White moorings are only for boats engaged in scuba diving. Red moorings are for boats engaged in snorkeling or more relaxed daytime cruising activities. These will usually be found in more sheltered or popular areas such as the *Rhone,* the Caves, or the Indians. Two blue buoys with a line and fishing floats between them are designated for dinghies. Tie the dinghy to the line between the buoys. These are currently at the *Rhone* and the Caves. Yachts must use these moorings and must have a BVI National Park Permit to use them. The fees help maintain the mooring system.

Because the British Virgin Islands has become such a popular cruising and diving area, the threat to the marine environment is increasing. Therefore it is important to follow practices of conservation carefully.

First, observe the rules of the marine parks and fisheries. The removal of any marine organism from BVI waters is illegal for non-British Virgin Islanders without a recreational fishing permit. Spearfishing, lobstering, or taking of live coral or live shells is prohibited. Strict penalties may be imposed.

The hawksbill turtle is one of the protected species often seen at dive sites in the BVI. (Photo: Odile Scheiner.)

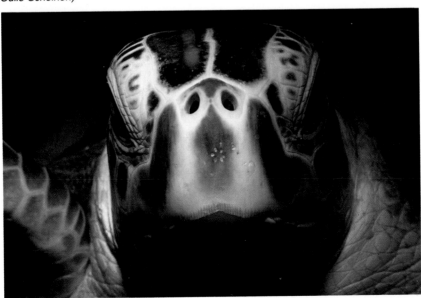

Mooring Etiquette

1. The diving and snorkeling moorings are for day-use ONLY. They are NOT the same as the moorings available in front of some restaurants. Honor the color coding system. The time limit on the yellow (commercial use only) or white (scuba diving only) buoys is 90 minutes. Once you have finished your dive, move off the mooring so that it is free for other boats coming to dive.

2. If you approach a mooring and it is occupied, inquire as to user's plans and either wait at a reasonable distance or choose another site. Do NOT anchor next to a mooring. That defeats the mooring system's purpose of protecting the fragile reef in the area.

3. Most moorings are only for boats up to 55 feet in length. A few sites have large yellow buoys indicating moorings for commercials boats over 55 feet.

4. When picking up a mooring, slip a 10- to 20-foot line through the eye of the pennant before securing it to your bow cleat. This will add additional scope and help prevent damage to the mooring. This is particularly important in areas prone to a lot of chop such as Alice in Wonderland, Blonde Rock, or the *Rhone.*

5. Should you damage a mooring, retrieve any salvageable parts and take them to the nearest commercial dive boat or shop. Be prepared to pay replacement costs.

6. Good seamanship suggests that before you leave your boat you inspect the mooring underwater and ensure that it shows no visual signs of damage. The moorings have a lot of use (and unfortunately, sometimes abuse). Use is at your own risk so caution and common sense are advised.

7. Prominently display a dive flag or the international code flag "A" while engaged in scuba on the moorings.

8. There are special rules for the RMS *Rhone* National Park:

   • No anchoring is allowed in the restricted area around the *Rhone*, which extends to and includes Dead Chest.
   • Yellow buoys are for commercial dive vessels only.
   • If all the moorings are full boats should use the Salt Island Settlement anchorage, arrive at the *Rhone* by tender, and use the moorings specified for dinghies.

Second, use common sense in anchoring and diving. Lower the anchor in a sand patch and make sure the anchor line is clear of coral when the boat swings. When diving, be aware of your body and avoid thrashing into coral. Photographers should exercise particular care as it easy to damage the reef when one's attention is focused thru the lens. When you make your approach for a photo and reach out to steady your body, carefully choose a piece of dead coral or a rock rather than a live organism.

If you choose to interact with the marine life, for instance, playing with an arrow crab, brittle star, or an eel, do so in a gentle manner respectful of its environment and experience. Patiently approach the cleaner shrimp and let him clean your hand rather than rip him from his home; quietly swim along side the eagle ray, slowing when he slows so he doesn't feel chased; remain quiet alongside a reef long enough for the fish to come to you rather than chase and frighten them away. Your experience will be richer for the respect you show the environment and the creatures in it. See "Diver's Guidelines for Protecting Reefs" on p. 82.

BVI dive operators have become increasingly concerned about conservation and support these practices. BVI Islanders understand that the natural environment is their most precious resource, and appreciate your help in preserving it. If you would like more information or want to join the Trust write: Friends of the National Parks Trust, Ministry of Natural Resources, Box 860, Road Town, Tortola, British Virgin Islands. You will receive a newsletter and support scientific research and conservation activity in the BVI.

This powerboat uses a mooring near the dive site at the Indians. These moorings are only for the use of boats while engaged in scuba diving. (Photo: Jim Scheiner.)

Boats entering anchorages should exercise care to find a sandy patch to drop the anchor in order to help preserve the delicate coral reef. (Photo: Jim Scheiner.)

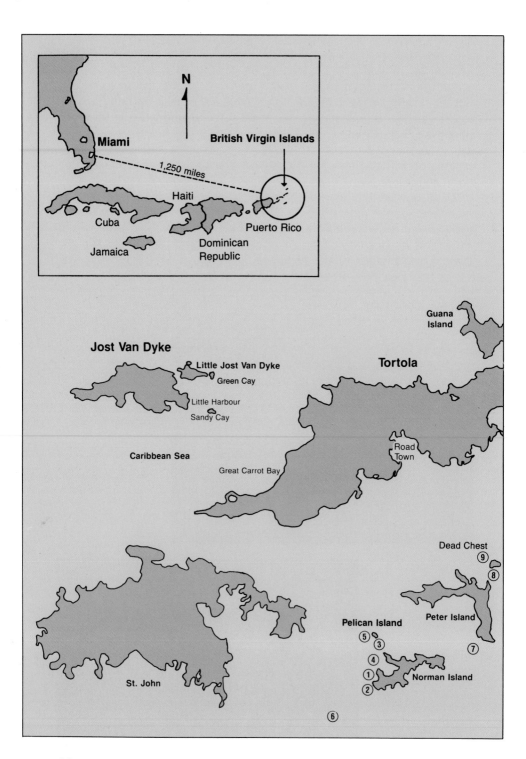

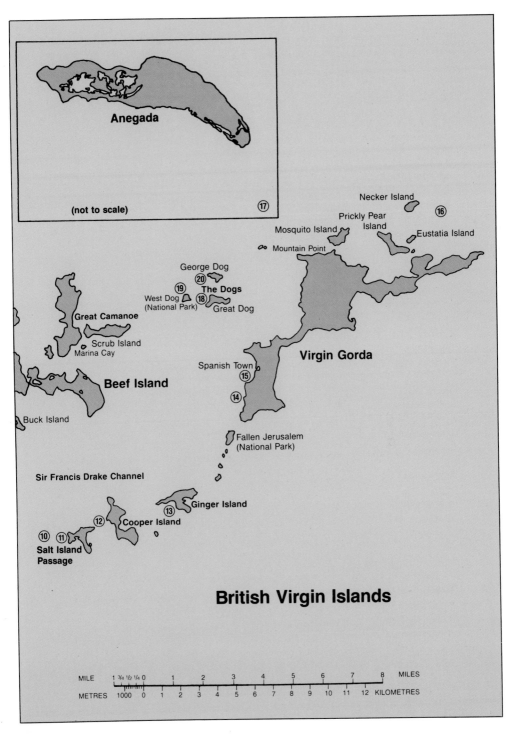

Anegada

(not to scale)

Necker Island

⑰

⑯

Prickly Pear Island

Mosquito Island

Eustatia Island

Mountain Point

George Dog

⑳

The Dogs

West Dog (National Park)

⑲

⑱

Great Dog

Great Camanoe

Scrub Island

Marina Cay

Spanish Town

Virgin Gorda

⑮

⑭

Beef Island

Buck Island

Fallen Jerusalem (National Park)

Sir Francis Drake Channel

Ginger Island

⑬

⑫

Cooper Island

⑩ ⑪

Salt Island Passage

British Virgin Islands

MILE 1 ¾ ½ ¼ 0   1   2   3   4   5   6   7   8   MILES

METRES 1000 0   1   2   3   4   5   6   7   8   9 10 11 12 KILOMETRES

Dive Site Ratings

	Novice Diver	Novice Diver and Instructor/Divemaster	Intermediate Diver	Intermediate Diver and Instructor/Divemaster	Advanced Diver	Advanced Diver and Instructor/Divemaster
Norman Island						
1 The Caves*						
2 Angelfish Reef			x	x	x	x
3 Rainbow Canyon	x	x	x	x	x	x
4 Ringdove Rock	x	x	x	x	x	x
5 The Indians*	x	x	x	x	x	x
6 Santa Monica Rock				x		x
Peter Island						
7 Carrot Shoal				x	x	x
8 Dead Chest West	x			x	x	x
9 Painted Walls				x	x	x
10 Blonde Rock				x	x	x
Salt Island						
11 Wreck of the RMS *Rhone* *				x	x	x
Cooper Island						
12 Dry Rocks West			x	x	x	x
Ginger Island						
13 Alice in Wonderland				x	x	x
Virgin Gorda						
14 The Baths*				x	x	x
15 The Aquarium	x	x	x	x	x	x
16 The Invisibles				x		x
Anegada						
17 Wreck of the *Rocus* *				x		x
The Dogs						
18 The Chimney*	x	x	x	x	x	x
19 Joe's Cave				x	x	x
20 Cockroach				x	x	x
21 Wreck of the *Chikuzen*				x		x

(* These areas offer excellent snorkeling, also)

3

Norman Island

Supposedly named after pirates and the island that inspired Robert Louis Stevenson to write *Treasure Island*, this still uninhabited island has long been associated with tales of buried treasure. A hoard was found in the caves at Treasure Point in 1907, which some believe belonged to Captain Kidd and others believe was the pirate Norman's. Another theory stems from a letter of 1750 mentioning recovery of "part of the treasure from the *Nuestra Señora* buried at Norman's Island, comprising $450,000, plate, cochineal, indigo, tobacco, . . ." The *Atlas of Treasure Maps* by F.L.Coffman, published in 1952, states "Norman Island . . . . has 120,000 pieces of eight buried and not recovered."

At one time a Norman Island Treasure Company engaged in an unsuccessful search for treasure, blasting holes throughout the island, which can still be seen today. The large anchorage at Norman has been named the "Bight" since pirate days because it has good holding, is well sheltered, and is wide enough for large sailing vessels to maneuver easily. For the same reasons many yachtsmen anchor there today. Awakening early in the morning to the cooing of the turtle doves, popping your head out the hatch, and seeing a square-rigged ship setting sail in the first light, it is easy to imagine yourself in another time and imagine that you might discover a pice of eight diving today.

Within a five-minute dinghy ride from the Bight lie several good, fairly calm dive sites with moorings: Angelfish Reef, Ringdove Rock, Rainbow Canyon, and the Indians. Only minutes away are The Caves, excellent for snorkeling. Santa Monica Rock is three quarters of a mile away and over open sea, so it is best visited with a guide.

Typical depth range:	4-40 feet
Typical current conditions:	None, but occasional surge
Expertise required:	Snorkeler
Access:	Boat

The caves lie just south of Treasure Point on the southwestern peninsula of Norman Island. Because there is as much to enjoy above the water as below, the caves are usually explored snorkeling. There are four caves, three of which you can swim into, with water about four feet deep. The southernmost cave has a bottom of rounded rocks on which you can stand. A skylight-like opening overhead illuminates the small room and the rich rust hues of the cave walls.

The second cave is a deep indentation in the rock face, rich in color above and below the water.

The third cave extends into the island about 80 feet. Take an underwater flashlight along to fully appreciate the brilliant purples, rusts, oranges, greens, and dark veins of the cave walls above the surface. Underwater, the experience is similar to a night dive, with polyps of coral extending

The southernmost cave at Norman Island invites exploration. It is easy to envision treasure buried in its recesses. (Photo: Linda Sorensen)

Snorkeling is the best way to enjoy the beauty above and below the water at the caves. (Photo: Allen Glenn.)

their tentacles. The walls are colored in red, blue, and yellow sponges. Once in the cave, let your eyes adjust to the darkness, and work your way towards a small room at the end of the tunnel.

The entrance to the fourth cave is above the water line and only for the adventurous who want to climb.

Outside the caves, schools of fry form moving shadows in the sparkling reef beauty. Yellow-tail snappers and sergeant majors abound, circling

A spiny oyster and closed cup coral decorate the walls of the Caves. (Photo: Jim Scheiner.)

This redspotted hawkfish perched on a sponge provides a challenging subject for the macro photographer. (Photo: Jim Scheiner.)

in a frenzy when snorkelers offer them food. Parrotfish, grouper, a resident puffer, and queen angels are usually seen around the coral and rocks. On the walls encrusted with fire coral you'll find red-lipped blennies, jewel-fish, small eels, and secretary blennies peering from the holes. From the sheer walls where the caves lie, the bottom drops quickly to 40 feet, and then slopes down to 65 feet. For the avid swimmer, there is good snor-keling from the Bight side of Treasure Point, south to the caves, along the ledge 150 feet off shore at Privateer Bay, and out to the southwestern tip of Privateer Bay. Watch for hawksbill turtles and eagle rays in the grassy areas of this bay.

It is easy to spend half or even a whole day enjoying the area around the caves, marveling at the underwater world, the rock formations, and the birdlife in the area, including pelicans, tropic birds, and laughing gulls. The area is generally calm in normal trade winds but sometimes a surge can wrap around the point. If it is surgy exercise care in entering the caves so as not to damage yourself or the delicate marine life. This is a popular spot so scuba is not advised due to the number of boats in the area and the abundance of other excellent dive sites nearby.

Angelfish Reef 2

Typical depth range:	10-90 feet
Typical current conditions:	None to moderate
Expertise required:	Intermediate
Access:	Boat

A lovely site off the Southwestern tip of Norman Island, Angelfish Reef has an abundance of fish life and excellent clarity due to the strong currents in the nearby channel. The rugged rocks that mark the point where the dive begins radiate outward underwater to a series of high ridges that create a maze of narrow canyons. The diver weaves through waving gorgonians, sea fans, and stands of elkhorn coral, and discovers

Clear water resulting from proximity to ocean currents enhances the beauty of the diving at Angelfish Reef. (Photo: Jim Scheiner.)

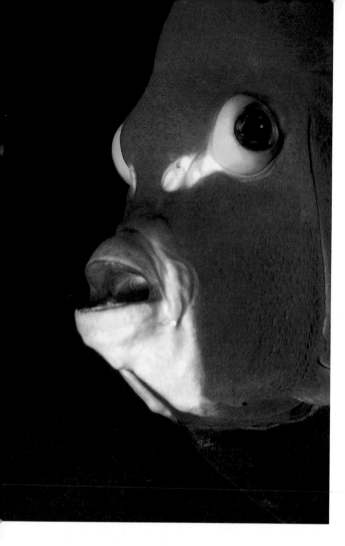

Angelfish are among the most curious fish on the reef. This French angelfish is just one of the species encountered at Angelfish Reef. (Photo: Jim Scheiner.)

spotted drums and high hats hiding under the same ledge accompanied by lingering schools of grunts. This is one of the few areas yellow-fin majora are seen, feeding in sand patches by thrusting its mouth into the sediment and expelling sand from its gills. French angels and queen angels thrive here, shyly displaying their beauty, as if enticing the diver to photograph them.

The reef slopes from 30 to 90 feet. Watch for amberjack, horse-eye jack, or a large school of palmeto. At depth, the water seems to turn a brighter blue and visibility increases. At the bottom of the channel huge sponges invite exploration and sting rays or eagle rays may silently appear, ghosting by with graceful sweeps of their wings, leaving the diver in awe as they swim away.

This site is just a few minutes by dinghy from Treasure Point and is a convenient scuba dive, while others in the party explore the caves.

Rainbow Canyon

Typical depth range:	20-50 feet
Typical current conditions:	None
Expertise required:	Novice with divemaster
Access:	Boat

Rainbow Canyon is a lovely spot off the southwest corner of Pelican Island. It is often used by local dive operations as a beginning dive, but offers interesting terrain for any level of diver. Among large mushroom-shaped coral heads, fire corals, brain coral, sea fans, gorgonians, and purple vase sponges, it is easy to find juvenile trunkfish, creole wrasse, chromis, angelfish, and squid. Try capturing a photo of the large trumpet-fish with a purple snout against the backdrop of a purple seafan or an elusive juvenile spotted drum.

The coral garden extends towards the rocks off Pelican and into canyon-like ridges that provide interesting exploration. Your guide can take you on a winding swim south of the point and over a saddle, leading back to the boat.

This shy juvenile spotted drum will develop spots along the dorsal fin as it matures. (Photo: Jim Scheiner.)

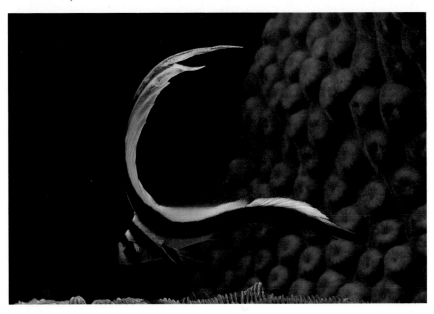

Typical depth range:	12-60 feet
Typical current conditions:	None to strong
Expertise required:	Novice with divemaster
Access:	Boat

A pinnacle about 150 feet across that comes within 12 feet of the surface, Ringdove Rock is west of the northwest arm of Norman Island. A navigational hazard, Ringdove was of more concern to the old square-rigger ships with their deep drafts as they sailed into the Bight than modern yachts with shallower drafts. Today, it is frequently visited for the pretty corals and lively fish activity.

From the surface descend toward the 60-foot bottom amid sea fans and gorgonians. Check under rocks for brilliant sponges, black and white

The Pederson shrimp lives in the protective tentacles of a spiral anemone. (Photo:Jim Scheiner.)

The abundance of sergeant majors at Ringdove Rock delight divers. Here a sergeant major valiantly guards purple masses of eggs on the vertical faces of rocks. (Photo: Linda Sorensen.)

spotted morays, and hiding rock beauties. Keep an eye toward the surrounding expanses of blue, as a turtle, ray, or large barracuda may come by to investigate.

As you circle Ringdove, you will come to a series of ridges on the west side that create good hiding places for fish. Yellow fire corals punctuated with swaying gorgonians and a remarkable abundance of darting sergeant majors create a beautiful reef scene. Watch for sergeant majors defending their purple egg masses clinging to vertical rock faces. When the sergeamt majors are unattentive for a fleeting moment, schools of female yellowhead wrasse and juvenile striped parrotfish move in for a frantic lunch until the sergeant major, reawakened to duty, darts in to chase them away. The scene of 200-300 sergeant majors patrolling the top of the reef against the deep blue backdrop makes a nice setting for diver shots.

Ringdove is a good place for fish photography, with an abundance of pretty tropicals such as foureye butterflyfish and reef butterflyfish. Be certain that your boat is marked with a dive flag in this area so sailors approaching the Bight will be alerted to watch for divers. Should you hear the sound of a propeller, stay down until it passes.

Typical depth range:	15-50 feet
Typical current conditions:	None to moderate, surge action at times
Expertise required:	Novice with divemaster
Access:	Boat

   North of Norman and west of Pelican Island four jagged pinnacles called the Indians jut dramatically above the water, high enough to be a significant landmark. There are several good dive sites in the area, the favorite right around the Indians. Clear, shallow areas on the east side of the Indians with good fish activity and pretty corals make it a favorite for snorkelers. However, when the wind is strong a surface current makes snorkeling here more challenging.

   Starting the dive on the west side of the northernmost Indian, the rock face forms a wall that drops to a bottom of 50 feet. Working south, the diver finds a variety of elkhorn, staghorn, brain, and star corals inter-

Divers enter the water from the live-aboard charter yacht Encore *as they begin a dive at the Indians. (Photo: Ann Glenn.)*

A small, goldentail moray eel, discovered while snorkeling, peeks its head from a hole in the fire coral in about ten feet of water at the Indians. (Photo: Linda Sorensen.)

A flamingo tongue graces the side of this purple seafan at the Indians. (Photo: Linda Sorensen.)

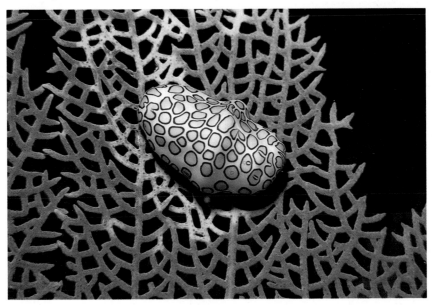

spersed with sea fans and gorgonians. Trumpetfish, angelfish, black durgons, blue chromis, rock beauties, and other tropicals abound. Reaching the east side of the Indians, there is a tunnel about 15 feet below the surface and 12 feet long that opens to a shallow basin. From here, divers swim west and explore a cave between two of the jutting rocks. Filled with an active school of glassy sweepers, this cave is a delight for the photographer. The fish are not inhibited by the diver and cooperatively swim back and forth, the light from another opening highlighting their shimmering bodies as they swim against the backdrop of colorful sponges and corals. The cave is large enough for several divers, but the magic is best experienced by one diver at a time.

The craggy outline of the rock formations here, the sparkling clarity of the shallow water, and the abundance of fish make this a delightful spot to explore. Look for purple and green or black and white flatworms in the shallow areas east of the Indians. Watch for lobster under the ledges and for small eels in the fire coral.

This is an excellent area for scuba photography and for snorkelers with the waterproof point and shoot cameras.

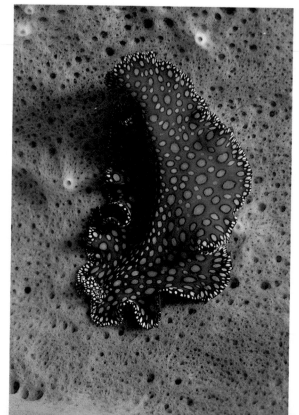

Delicate, colorful flatworms are easily found at the Indians. (Photo: Jim Scheiner.)

Santa Monica Rock 6

Typical depth range:	11-70 feet
Typical current conditions:	Moderate to strong
Expertise required:	Intermediate with divemaster
Access:	Boat

Santa Monica Rock is a large underwater pinnacle three fourths of a mile southwest of the southwest point of Norman Island. The top of the pinnacle is approximately 100 yards in diameter and 11 feet deep; the base is about 400 yards in diameter at 70 feet deep. The area is so extensive that this pinnacle easily warrants several dives to explore it thoroughly. Because

Hawksbill turtles are often found hiding under ledges at Santa Monica Rock. (Photo: Nancy Ferguson)

A swift school of African pompano swim from the open sea. (Photo: Jim Scheiner.)

this site is so close to the open ocean, visibility is excellent, often exceeding 125 feet.

The top of Santa Monica is covered with stony corals and lush gorgonians. There is an abundance of reef fish such as grouper, angelfish, and black durgons. As the diver works down the pinnacle, there are ledges, caves, and holes to explore and ridges of rock radiating outward. It is not unusual to find a green moray, a hawksbill turtle, or see schools of spadefish, chub, horse-eye jack, or barracuda. On the south and east sides the pinnacle drops almost vertically from 20 to 50 feet. A parade of passing pelagic fish and the sense of being so far out toward the open sea keep the diver alert and his senses heightened.

Santa Monica is not particularly easy for the newcomer to find, so it is best to visit the site with an experienced guide. If the wind is up, surface conditions can be rough, so try to time your visit on a calm day.

4

Peter Island

Carrot Shoal   7

Typical depth range:	11-60 feet
Typical current conditions:	None to moderate but can be surface chop from wind
Expertise required:	Intermediate with divemaster
Access:	Boat

Carrot Shoal is a 200-foot ridge rising from 60 feet of water to within 11 feet of the surface just two fifths of a mile west southwest of Carrot Rock. Close to the open sea, Carrot Shoal is usually an exciting dive with good clarity. There are many crannies for fish to hide in, overhanging ledges and one particularly pretty archway, often with a resident nurse

The graceful silhouette of two French angels at Carrot Shoal. (Photo: Linda Sorensen.)

shark resting beneath it. Near the top, bright with yellow fire coral, there is an abundance of colorful tropicals. Along the walls of the pinnacle watch for large midnight parrotfish, snappers, schoolmasters, Spanish grunts, barracuda, and black durgons. Poke under the ledges looking for lobster or eels, or sunburst anemone in cracks and crevices.

This site is exposed to the wind and currents from the southeast trades, so it is best to choose a calmer day for comfort in the diveboat.

Found only in the darkest crevices of reefs and wrecks, the sunburst anemone is a rare and stunningly beautiful treat for the lucky night diver. Extending its tentacles from a central oral disc only after nightfall and entirely curling them inward again once a diver's light shines upon this creature, the sunburst anemone is difficult to spot and even more of a challenge to photograph.

This colorful creature survives on a diet of fishes, oysters, and crabs. Sweeping its tentacles out towards its prey, the prey is seized, stung, and swallowed with lightning speed. The sunburst anemone can engulf a fish almost the size of its own body column.

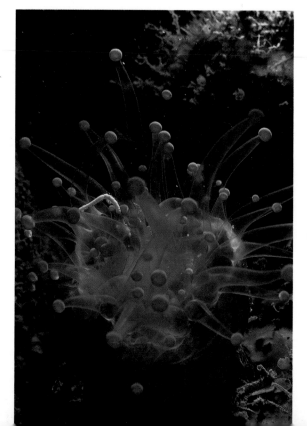

The sunburst (or orange ball) anemone reveals its beauty only after dark and quickly retreats when exposed to light. It can sense movement and reaches out to capture its prey with its orange tipped tentacles. (Photo: Jim Scheiner.)

Typical depth range:	20-50 feet
Typical current conditions:	None, surface chop from wind when strong
Expertise required:	Novice with divemaster
Access:	Boat

Dead Chest West is an interesting site along the coral reef just south of Dead Chest, half a mile off Peter Island. Reputedly the island where Blackbeard left 15 men with a bottle of rum and a sabre to fight out their differences, it is easy to imagine some of the pirates deciding to swim the half a mile to Dead Man's Bay on Peter Island. Perhaps the name signifies the unsuccessful outcome of such attempts.

Immediately under the boat, when using the mooring over the site, is an archway where small spotted lobsters and fairy basslets are found. Nearby there are spur and groove formations, rows of sandy strips alternating with rows of rock and coral, all enlivened with brightly colored

Dead Chest West is a good place to observe the habits of small reef creatures such as these two dueling sailfin blennies. (Photo: Jim Scheiner.)

Lettuce sea slugs, such as the one on this red sponge, are vegetarians and can be found at Dead Chest West. (Photo: Jim Scheiner.)

tropicals. Multi-colored sponges and cup corals thrive along undercut ledges and overhangs. An excellent site for macro photography, look for banded coral shrimp, decorator crabs hiding in vase sponges, secretary blennies peering from fire coral covered homes, and lacy, white, hard corals. When you reach an area of small boulders, search carefully for baby slipper lobster, brittle stars, tiny transparent flatworms, or black and white flatworms, all excellent macro subjects.

A triangular opening in a fissure in the cliff forms a cave where glassy sweepers create clouds of shimmering movement. Around the corner is a cave in a hollowed out boulder, where a big green moray eel surveys the reef scene.

In the early '80s a big freighter was grounded near this site. Unfortunately, in the salvage operation towing cables managed to wipe out big swatches of the coral reef. However, it is interesting to see the process of a reef slowly reestablishing itself. First the algaes take hold, then the sponges and grasses, next the soft corals and finally, slowly, the hard corals. It will be years before this damaged area is renewed to the beauty around it, but it is interesting to observe the process.

The average depth of Dead Chest is about 35 feet, and it is a beautiful place for exploration and photography, the kind of dive you can take your time to investigate and enjoy.

Typical depth range:	20-50 feet
Typical current conditions:	Little to strong with occasional surge
Expertise required:	Intermediate with divemaster
Access:	Boat

The Painted Walls is a spectacular dive site on the southeast corner of Dead Chest off Peter Island. A rocky ridge, partially awash in foaming surf, juts southward into the open sea. Dive boats use the mooring established by the BVI National Trust or anchor west of the ridge.

The dive starts under the boat, where there is an abundance of hard corals, soft gorgonians, sponges, and colorful fish. Working toward the point, excellent visibility, often more than 100 feet, enchances the liveliness and beauty of the reef. Queen angelfish weave around stands of pillar coral, sea fans, and fire coral. It is not unusual to see a hawksbill turtle, a ray, or an occasional shark.

On the seaward side there are three vertical canyons, the largest about 40 by 120 feet, and immediately it is apparent why this site is named the Painted Walls. The vertical formations of rock are completely covered with an array of sponges and cup corals, artistry gone wild with color — brilliant yellow, crimson red, blue, white, and orange. Flame scallops, spiny oysters, and Christmas tree worms tuck themselves into the display. There is so much to see that it is tempting to linger, but it is necessary to keep moving to complete the circuit on one tank of air. Be sure to look under one of the polished round rocks that comprise the floor of these brilliant rooms and find wiggly brittle starfish hiding there.

A small decorator crab carries sponges on its shell for disguise. This crab was found inside a vase sponge. (Photo: Linda Sorensen.)

Two rough file shells and encrusting sponges are typical of the abundance of colorful growth on the vertical surfaces of the Painted Walls.. (Photo: Linda Sorensen.)

Tentacles polyps of cup coral fully extended to capture food particles in the water enhance the beauty of the Painted Walls. (Photo: Jim Scheiner.)

This small octopus slithers over sponges as he returns to his hiding place. (Photo: Jim Scheiner.)

From the head of the second canyon a beautiful tunnel about 10 feet long leads to a shallow reef behind the walls. From there meander through more of the extensive coral garden patches, lingering to watch parrotfish, banded butterfly fish, creole wrasse, or stands of pillar coral as you make your way back to the boat.

Photo tips. Due to the clarity of the water, abundance of tropical fish, and dramatic topography, almost any lense format has excellent potential here. The walls provide a macro photographer's paradise. Or, with a wide angle lens, try shots of divers framed by the tunnel, either in silhouette or with flash to illuminate faces and the brilliant colors of the sponges.

Typical depth range:	10-60 feet
Typical current conditions:	Slight to strong, surface chop if wind is strong
Expertise required:	Intermediate with divemaster
Access:	Boat

About one third of the way from Dead Chest on a line toward Salt Island lies a patch of yellow fire coral atop a rock pinnacle, obvious from the surface in good light. From this patch of yellow, ranging from 9 to 12 feet deep, comes the name Blonde Rock. The pinnacle area is about 300 feet across, with the sides dropping to a white sandy bottom at 60 feet.

As the diver enters the water and descends below the fire coral, he or she is greeted with waving fields of soft gorgonians, seawhips, purple seafans, and brain coral. Descending further, he reaches the most prominent feature of Blonde Rock, a vertical coral ledge that weaves along the eastern side of the reef. Deeply undercut, it forms a series of coral caves and crevices and is covered with flowering cup corals in brilliant shades of orange and yellow. The diver peeking into nooks in search of

Scrawled file fish such as this one are often seen swimming in pairs at Blonde Rock. (Photo: Jim Scheiner.)

A school of French grunts linger under a ledge at Blonde Rock. (Photo: Nancy Ferguson.)

a lobster or eel will emerge, look up and see the ragged shape of overhanging ledges against shimmering surface waters. Take a wide angle lens if you want to capture images of divers against colorful coral outcroppings.

The sense of being under the ledge as if half in a cave, exploring the secrets of marine life along this undercut wall, make this dive unique. Photographers with a close-up format will single out the glasseye snapper, a nocturnal fish, spending his day stationary under a ledge. French angels, queen angels, scrawled filefish, rock beauties, puffers, and damselfish also make this magic place home.

As you return to the shallower areas at the end of the dive, watch for schools of sennets, horse-eyed jacks, and bluestriped grunts. This area attracts pelagics and the feeling of a world in motion dominates as schools of fish quickly swim by. The top of the reef is colorful, sparkling with tropicals.

5

Salt Island

The Wreck of the RMS *Rhone*

Typical depth range:	30-80 feet
Typical current conditions:	None to strong, can change quickly
Expertise required:	Intermediate with divemaster
Access:	Boat

The wreck of the *Rhone* has practically become synonomous with the BVI, and most traveling divers know of the *Rhone* from the wide publicity she has received. Even those who are not divers may have seen the *Rhone* in Columbia Pictures' treasure diving drama, *The Deep*. Regarded as one

The bow of the Rhone *lies in 70-80 feet of water. The 310-foot Royal Mail Steam Ship sunk off Salt Island during a hurricane in 1867. (Photo: Jim Scheiner.)*

Parts of the Rhone *are heavily encrusted with corals and attract a variety of reef fish. (Photo: Jim Scheiner.)*

of the best wreck dives in the Caribbean, a visit to the *Rhone* is a highlight of a diving trip to the BVI.

A 310-foot sailing steamer built in England for the Royal Mail Steam Packet Company in 1865, the *Rhone* was a handsome vessel and known as one of the most advanced forms of marine transportation of her time. With a beam of 40 feet and 2,738 gross registered tons, she had 253 first-class, 30 second-class, and 30 third-class cabins. During her brief career, she transported cargo and passengers to ports throughout the West Indies and South America.

Anchored at Great Harbor, Peter Island on the morning of October 29, 1867, the RMS *Rhone* was taking on cargo and stores for a return trip to England. About 11 a.m. the barometer fell suddenly to 27.95 in.Hg, the sky darkened, and hurricane winds from the north-northwest hit the hull and tore at the rigging. With engines running at full speed ahead, she weathered the first half of the tempest.

At noon, there was a lull. In an attempt to seek searoom to weather the second half of the storm, the captain decided to steam seaward. With engines at full speed, the *Rhone* passed through the channel between Salt and Peter Island. Just as she was almost to sea, hurricane force winds from the south-southeast struck, forcing her onto the rocks at Salt Island.

Looking out from the interior of the bow section of the Rhone *a diver is silhouetted. (Photo: Jim Scheiner.)*

She heeled over, broke in two, and sunk immediately. Only one passenger and a few crew members survived.

Today, her two halves are well preserved on a sandy bottom and her steel wreckage is home to encrusting corals and a variety of species of fish. The *Rhone* is ideal for a two-tank dive. The bow section, about 150 feet long, lies in 70-80 feet of water. The diver can swim inside the bow section and is greeted by schools of fish in the cargo hold and coral encrusted interior chambers. Outside, the bowsprit and the foremast with crow's nest virtually intact lie in the sand. One of the *Rhone*'s two cannons can be seen pinned beneath the wreckage at 70 feet.

South of the bow section, the boilers, the condenser, a complete set of large open end wrenches, a winch, and water pump lie scatterd over the sand. Schools of snappers, grunts and horse-eye jacks swim around the wreckage at the midsection.

The stern section, often done as a second dive, lies in 30 feet of water with the rudder extending upward to within 15 feet of the surface. The huge propellor, battered during the fatal collision into Black Rock Point, once drove the *Rhone* at a top speed of 14 knots. Also notice the boilers, the gear box housing, the long propeller shaft, and the aft mast lying parallel to the stern section.

A wide variety of fish species live among the coral encrusted wreckage. Sergeant majors, blue runners, and yellowtail snapper looking for food handouts greet the diver. Blackbar soldierfish live inside the bow, angelfish grace the wreck with their elegant silhouettes, and gray snapper, black durgon, parrotfish, squirrelfish, Spanish hogfish, and grunts are easily spotted. Also watch for eels, turtles, and barracuda.

The *Rhone* and surrounding area was declared a National Park in 1980. Spearfishing, linefishing, taking of coral, shells, artifacts, or anchoring

Colorful tropicals such as this French angel grace the wreck. (Photo: Jim Scheiner.)

The propeller once drove the Rhone *at 14 knots. Today the stern lies in 15-30 feet of water. (Photo: Jim Scheiner.)*

over the wreck is strictly prohibited. Special moorings have been established; some for the use of commercial dive vessels only, others for visiting dive vessels, and some for dinghy use. Because of the high traffic in the area, it is important to observe the rules, maneuver with extreme caution, and watch carefully for divers in the water. Once your dive is complete, move off the mooring to free it for another party. With more than 100 divers visiting the *Rhone* on many days, it is particularly important to exercise care underwater to preserve the delicate marine life. Watch your buoyancy control and avoid touching corals as much as possible. (See Chapter 2 on Mooring Etiquette and Conservation.)

Divers and non-divers can enjoy an "aerial" view of the *Rhone* site by snorkeling over the area. Beware of the surface current and boats in the area.

To maximize your dive, it is suggested that you go with an experienced local diving professional. He or she can orient you to the dive site, point out the major features of the *Rhone* underwater, and provide knowledgeable surface support in assessing current conditions and traffic complications. Once you dive the *Rhone* you'll experience first hand why this wreck has become such a popular site and still creates a sense of mystery for those who have explored her depths countless times.

6

Cooper Island

Dry Rocks West   12

Typical depth range:	25-40 feet
Typical current conditions:	None to strong (areas can be unswimmable)
Expertise required:	Intermediate
Access:	Boat

Also called "Vanishing Rocks," these rocks awash are located off the northeastern point of Salt Island, approximately on a line with Cistern point on Cooper Island. Because strong currents flow through the area,

A diver amidst gorgonians and star coral watches two butterflyfish at Dry Rocks West. (Photo: Linda Sorensen.)

This school of longspine squirrelfish at Dry Rock West are chiefly active at night. Their large eyes allow them to see better in the dark. (Photo: Jim Scheiner.)

there is a remarkable abundance of coral and fish life. Undercut ledges of rock covered in brilliant sponges, schools of French grunts milling around beautiful brain corals, stately seafans, and flowing gorgonians all set the stage for excellent photographic ventures. A large stand of pillar coral with bright tropicals playing in the branches is particularly notable. Watch for a trio of reef butterflyfish, trumpetfish, Spanish hogfish, lobster, or a nurse shark. The relatively shallow depths give you time to circle the rocks and enjoy the colorful abundance of marine life. Swim by Sergeant Major City, where schools of this frisky fish circle impetuously, adding their flair to the beauty of the reef.

7

Ginger Island

Typical depth range:	40-80 feet
Typical current conditions:	None to light, surface chop common
Expertise required:	Intermediate
Access:	Boat

On the south side of the western arm of Ginger Island lies South Bay, generally exposed to the southeast trades, and therefore usually a rough anchorage. However, it is the site of a magical dive and if you are willing

Dramatic mushroom-shaped star corals, large seafans and clear water are typical of Alice in Wonderland diving. (Photo: Linda Sorensen.)

Blue chromis dot a stand of pillar coral and colorful sponges line the underside of coral heads at Ginger Island. (Photo: Linda Sorensen.)

to tolerate a bit of topside chop or wait for a calm day, you can experience the wonders of Alice in Wonderland.

Descending to 50 feet the diver finds himself among stands of huge mushroom shaped star corals, 10 to 15 feet high with white sand valleys running between them. There is a sense of being in a maze, a diver shrunk in size alongside the statuesque coral of a fantasy world. You can almost envision one of Lewis Carrolls' caterpillars perched atop one of these magnificent heads, puffing a pipe, musing about life.

Large purple and green seafans, soft gorgonians, and pillar coral add to the scene. The underneath sides of the mushroom-shaped corals are encrusted with brilliant sponges that add highlights to photos taken here. Blue chromis and yellowhead wrasse sprinkle the corals with motion and color. Banded butterfly fish and snout nose butterfly fish are attractive subjects for the photographer. African pompano may swim by, and this is a good place to sight large grouper, rays, reef sharks, or even jewfish. Once you've been to Alice's enticing coral garden, you may never want to leave.

8

Virgin Gorda

The Baths   14

Typical depth range:	5-30 feet
Typical current conditions:	None, surge can be strong, waves breaking on beach
Expertise required:	Snorkeler or intermediate diver
Access:	Boat or beach

Along with the *Rhone* and the Caves, the Baths is one of the most visited sites in the British Virgin Islands. A spectacular collection of giant boulders strewn across palm lined white beaches on the southwestern end

A peacock flounder can disguise himself by changing hues according to his background. They are frequently seen in the sand around the Baths. (Photo: Jim Scheiner.)

Stoplight parrotfish have strong teeth and eat coral, which is then digested and contributes to the sand-making process. (Photo: Jim Scheiner.)

of Virgin Gorda, this natural wonder is beautiful both above and below the water, and well worth setting aside a day to climb, explore, and rediscover the pleasures of snorkeling.

These huge boulders are randomly tumbled upon one another, creating secret rooms, pools, cracks, and crevices in a variety of interesting shapes. Some areas are hollowed out by the erosion of wind and sea, creating honeycomb effects, like giant beehives in the rock. The roots of strangler figs hang like vines into the cool shade of hidden rooms and shafts of light from open crevices overhead illuminate pools of shimmering water.

Geologists speculate that these granite monoliths were formed when molten rock seeped into existing volcanic layers of rock. Because this happened below the surface of the earth, the molten rock cooled slowly, forming hard crystalline granite layers. Shrinkage and cracking formed blocks that were exposed when the softer volcanic rock eroded away. These boulders were then weathered by wind and water to form the rounded formations seen today.

The snorkeling is excellent around the Baths. The dramatic shapes create interesting spaces underwater for fish to hide and coral to grow.

The entrance to one of the most popular series of cave-like room lies in the shadow of this giant boulder. (Photo: Jim Scheiner.) ▶

Various sizes and shapes of granite boulders are strewn across the beaches at the Baths. A visit here is a highlight of a trip to the BVI. (Photo: Jim Scheiner.)

The whiteness of the sand reflects light upward and enhances the water's sparkling clarity. From the Baths around to Spring Bay or Devil's Bay, weave in and out of giant boulders, look for caves, and investigate under coral ledges. Observe jewelfish with their diamond studded blue bodies hiding in elkhorn coral, watch for peacock flounder or sting rays gliding over ripples in the sand, and see large blue parrotfish nibbling coral.

Because the Baths is so popular with yachtsmen and swimmers, boats are required to anchor west of a line of marker buoys, about 100 yards offshore. A marked channel allows dinghies access to the beach. Swimmers and snorkelers should stay out of the channel and east of the anchoring limit. This is the area along the beach and boulders where the best snorkeling is found.

In the winter there can frequently be a surge at the Baths, especially when the north swell is running. Boaters may then prefer to go to Virgin Gorda Yacht Harbor at Spanish Town and approach the Baths by taxi and footpath. When the waves are large, the complexion of the Baths changes dramatically. Instead of peaceful snorkeling, you have the chance to see the Baths in another mood — the dramatic splendor of waves crashing against these rocks and foaming into the inner pools and spaces, spewing spray high into the air.

When conditions are calm, and you want to scuba dive this area, you may want to explore a particularly lovely cave on the south side of Devil's Bay in 12 to 15 feet of water. Glassy sweepers and gray snapper illuminated by shafts of light sway in the surge. Cup corals and encrusting sponges decorate the walls. This is a shallow, pretty dive, good for the photographer content to work one area. Dive only near the rocks and *do not* dive in the area where boats may be anchoring or maneuvering.

Typical depth range:	15-30 feet
Typical current conditions:	None
Expertise required:	Novice with divemaster
Access:	Boat

Just off Fort Point, near Spanish Town and less than a mile north of the Baths, lies a broad area of underwater boulders and corals, some only 9 feet below the surface. The Aquarium, also called Fischer's Rocks, is an excellent easy dive with an abundance of fish. Due to the shallow depths, lack of current, and active fish life, this is often used as a beginner's dive, but one that any diver can appreciate.

Hard corals, sea fans, and gorgonians are scattered among the boulders, with fire coral, cup corals, and sponges flourishing on the rocks. Milling schools of French grunts, sergeant majors, and blue tangs set the reef in motion, while colorful anemones hide cleaner shrimp and arrow crabs.

This porcupinefish hiding under a ledge underlined with red sponges is accompanied by sergeant majors. Puffers gulp water to inflate themselves for protection, and are often seen at the Aquarium. (Photo: Nancy Ferguson)

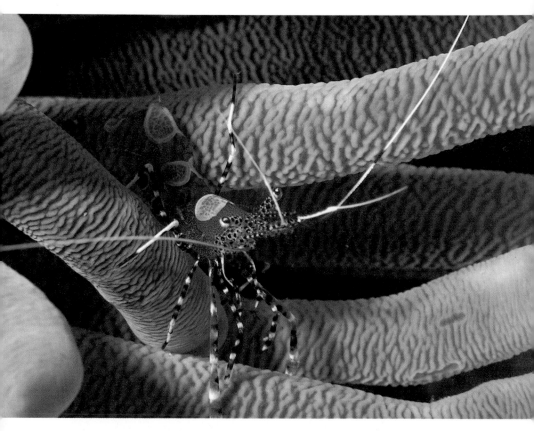

A spotted cleaning shrimp awaits atop the tip of a tentacle for a fish to stop for cleaning. (Photo: Nancy Ferguson.)

Beginning divers will delight to see their first reef squid, puffers, small eels, barracuda, nurse shark, or meet the 8-foot-long green moray.

When diving this site, it is important to use a boat well marked as a dive boat, as there is a lot of yachting traffic between the Yacht Harbor and the Baths.

Typical depth range:	16-60 feet
Typical current conditions:	None to strong, surface chop can be very rough when wind is strong
Expertise required:	Intermediate or advanced with guide
Access:	Boat

North of Virgin Gorda, one mile east of Necker Island, several rocky pinnacles rise from 60 feet of water to within 4 and 8 feet of the surface. The site is difficult to find and the boat trip to the site from Virgin Gorda can be a rough one, so it is best to go with a guide who knows the area, preferably on a calm day. Yet, because these pinnacles are so exposed,

If the diver is lucky, he may spot a jewfish, creatures that weight up to 700 pounds. (Photo: Jim Scheiner.)

The Invisibles serve as a beacon to passing pelagics such as these Atlantic spadefish. (Photo: Jim Scheiner.)

they act as a beacon to passing pelagic fish. Divers visit the Invisibles with a sense of adventure, watching for the unexpected.

Entering the water, you descend below the turbulence of the surface into a world of archways, caves and crevices created by a jumble of rocks around the pinnacles. Appearing immediately are black durgons, their dark bodies outlined by crisp white lines. A queen triggerfish nibbles at a sea urchin, and a large grouper awaits motionless at a cleaning station. Under the ledges you can find large lobsters or puffers, whose large eyes intently focus on you. Brilliantly colored sponges and cup corals cling to the shaded areas of the rocks, a beautiful backdrop for the busy activity of angelfish, squirrelfish, and schools of grunts.

Some dives reveal a large green moray, with its mouth open, slowly emerging from a coral head, or a shark whose sluggish movements belie its smooth skin and strength. Horse-eye jacks investigate visitors from the surface, and you might even see a jewfish if you scan your surroundings for these large shapes. Spadefish, with their graceful presence and diffuse vertical stripes dissolve into the scene. Time seems to stop, as you feel like an integral part of this underwater world. When your bottom time is up, you'll return reluctantly to the surface, already anticipating the next time you can dive the Invisibles.

9

Anegada

In contrast to the other mountainous volcanic islands of the BVI, Anegada is a flat coral and limestone island with its highest point at 28 feet. Nine miles long, it is fringed with sandy beaches. Horseshoe Reef extends 10 miles to the southeast and has claimed more than 300 known wrecks. Over the years numerous treasure hunting adventurers have sought to unlock the secrets of these now coral encrusted ships. The same hazards that claimed these wrecks continue to make navigating near Anegada tricky today. It is wise to travel near the reef only in good light and favorable weather. Any trip to Anegada carries with it an aura of danger and mystery.

Proposals to temporarily restrict anchoring in the Anegada Reef area have been made by the Department of Fisheries and Wildlife to preserve the reef habitat and natural nursery that the reef creates. Check with local dive shops on current policy before venturing to Anegada.

Wreck of the *Rocus* 17

Typical depth range:	40 feet
Typical current conditions:	None to strong, usually surgy
Expertise required:	Intermediate with guide
Access:	Boat

Nine miles from the tip of Anegada, near the end of Horseshoe Reef lies the 380-foot Greek freighter *Rocus*, which sank in 1929. The steel ship was traveling from Trinidad to Baltimore heavily loaded with a cargo of cattle bones to be made into bone meal fertilizer. An unfortunate error in navigation brought her to her current resting place.

Today, the wreck is a twisted mass of broken steel lying on her side in 40 feet of water. The aft section is mostly intact and the large curve

A diver explores the shallow water of the wreck of the Rocus *which sank in 1929. The area is still littered with cattle bones, part of the ship's cargo. (Photo: Nancy Ferguson)*

of the stern creates an arch that makes an excellent photo prop. Cattle bones and machinery litter the ocean floor. Large boilers, measuring 20 feet in diameter, the engine, winches, and capstan are still intact. The bow is in shallow water and breaks in a heavy sea.

Elkhorn and other hard corals surround the *Rocus*, a home for schooling fry and reef fish. Black jacks, black durgons, a large green moray, and nurse sharks are often seen here. The dive is shallow and often surgy, but the abundance of fish life on this remote and eerie wreck provides an excellent photographic setting.

Local knowledge is necessary to navigate the reef and to locate the wreck. Approach should be made only in good light.

◀ *The common crawfish or spiny lobster can be found at the* Rocus. *(Photo: Jim Scheiner.)*

10

The Dogs

The Chimney 18

Typical depth range:	25-50 feet
Typical current conditions:	None, surge at times can be dangerous
Expertise required:	Novice with divemaster
Access:	Boat

On the north side of the west bay of Great Dog are a series of rocky cliffs. Exploring the area underwater the diver swims into a wide arched tunnel. The walls here are thickly covered with yellow and orange cup corals and white sponges, interspersed with red and blue sponges, wispy hydroids, and delicate, white lacy corals. At the other end of this room-like tunnel the overhead opens to the surface and two large rocks stand closely spaced together. The dive is named the Chimney after this formation.

Queen angels often adorn the narrow slot of the Chimney, and on the reef outside fish play in stands of coral and gorgonians. Watch for trunkfish, spotted drums, Spanish grunts, and an occasional nurse shark.

When there is no north swell, this is a comfortable and easy dive but if the swell is up, the narrow slot of the Chimney can be dangerous and it is best to choose another dive site.

A well framed photograph requires more than composition and color—it often requires a patient friend, too! (Photo: Jim Scheiner.) ▶

Extended yellow polyps of cup coral and white sponges grace the entrance to the Chimney. (Photo: Linda Sorensen.)

Typical depth range:	20-30 feet
Typical current conditions:	None to slight, surge action with north swell
Expertise required:	Intermediate with divemaster
Access:	Boat

On the northwest side of West Dog lies a 30–40-foot deep cathedral-like cave carved into the rock both above and below the water's surface. Inside, schools of glassy sweepers and clouds of silversides add motion to the dramatic setting colored with sponges and cup corals. Large rocks outside the cave and around the northern point hide lobster, puffers and a variety of eels. Watch for a fleeting glimpse of tarpon with jutting jaws, large scales, and a powerful swim, that disappear as quickly as they appear. On the sandy bottom watch rays bury themselves in the sand and nurse sharks resting under ledges.

This site was named after the owner of a diving operation who explored this area. Joe's Cave is best explored when there is no north swell running.

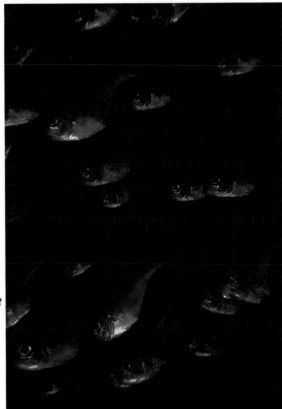

Clouds of glassy sweepers create glimmers of movement at Joe's Cave. (Photo: Linda Sorensen.)

A spotted moray eel hides behind an anemone at Joe's Cave. (Photo: Jim Scheiner.)

Typical depth range:	12-70 feet
Typical current conditions:	None to very strong
Expertise required:	Intermediate with divemaster
Access:	Boat

About 100 yards off the southwest corner of Cockroach Island lies a rocky pinnacle about 12 feet below the surface. To the west the pinnacle drops to a bottom of 70 feet, to the east a ridge of rocks creating canyons, archways, and crevices extends towards Cockroach. This dive usually begins with the boat anchored or moored to the east of the pinnacle. Because the current can be strong on the surface, it is best for divers to descend on the anchor or mooring line until they reach some lee from the rocks on the bottom.

Cockroach is one of the most beautiful and exciting dives in the area. The coral growth is so lush it seems to cover every square inch of rock. The coral encrusted rocks teem with colorful reef fish and pelagic varieties cruise the site. The same current that can make Cockroach challenging to divers also brings in nutrients that contribute to the abundance of life in the area.

At Cockroach every inch of the rocks seem to be covered with coral, sponges, or gorgonians. (Photo: Linda Sorensen.)

Eight reef butterflyfish hungrily consume purple sergeant major eggs while the guarding parent is distracted from his protective duties. (Photo: Linda Sorensen.)

The top section of the pinnacle is covered with fire coral where active sergeant majors, bluehead wrasse, and creole wrasse play. Occasionally a stately orange filefish makes her presence here, a peculiar subject for the photographer. Sergeant majors defiantly defend their patches of purple eggs. If their attention lapses for a moment, a group of greedy reef butterflyfish move in to devour all they can until run off by the valiant defender.

Descending deeper, you'll see snapper, grouper, and squirrelfish milling about. The undersides of the ledges are heavily encrusted with bright sponges and corals. On the seaward side rays, turtles, schools of spadefish or jacks, and an occasional shark may be seen. Eels and lobster are often found in the crevices.

After diving the deep section, if time and air allow, (well worth a second tank), there is a wonderland to explore in the ridge extending from the pinnacle toward Cockroach Island. Angelfish frequent this maze of canyons and crevices and, if the photographer is patient enough, will swim through one of the arches creating a perfect framing for the graceful silhouettes. The walls of the canyons are thick with brilliant sponges and excellent macro subjects. Gorgonians, sea fans, and anenomes soften the bottom, creating hiding places for trumpetfish and schools of goatfish.

Typical depth range:	40-75 feet
Typical current conditions:	None to strong
Expertise required:	Intermediate with divemaster
Access:	Boat

The *Chikuzen* is one of the BVI's outstanding dive sites. It is tricky to find, located out in the open sea 9½ miles northwest of Mountain Point, Virgin Gorda, and the trip is best made in settled weather. But with an experienced guide to locate the site, the *Chikuzen* can be a superb experience.

Once a 246-foot steel hulled Japanese refrigeration ship used in the long line fishing trade, in more recent years the *Chikuzen* served as a warehouse at the dock in St. Martin. Her useful life mostly spent, she was taken to sea to sink, but instead remained afloat and drifted 70 miles to the BVI. When her cumbersome hulk appeared headed for BVI shores, she was towed farther out to sea and finally sank in 75 feet of water. She came to rest on her port side on a sandy bottom in September 1981 and

Schools of circling amberjacks greet the diver at the Chikuzen, *adding to the excitement of the dive. (Photo: Jim Scheiner.)*

Drooping lines of the rigging around the mast and crow's nest at the Chikuzen are accompanied with a symphony of fish movement. (Photo: Jim Scheiner.)

The 246-foot Chikuzen lies on its port side in 75 feet of water nine miles from any island. (Photo: Jim Scheiner.)

An abundance of schooling fish is characteristic of a dive at the Chikuzen. *(Photo: Jim Scheiner.)*

almost immediately began to attract reef and pelagic life. She is now home to schools of amberjack and horse-eye jacks, barracuda, grunts, snapper, spadefish, eagle and sting rays, and even an occasional shark or jewfish.

As you descend toward the wreck, you are greeted with perhaps a hundred barracuda, like an armed guard choosing to escort you to the site. Soon, large schools of amberjack appear, swiftly swimming up to and around the diver as you descend the anchor line. Reaching the white bottom, you may spot a large sting ray lying motionless half covered in sand. Investigating the wreck, and looking into the refrigeration hold, you'll discover it's alive with schools of fish. Outside, the rigging draped from the mast and crow's nest gives an eerie feel to the scene. Swim along the deck, around the bow and along the hull, then back to the stern. You might see an octopus dart from her hiding place and dance across the hull, changing colors as she goes. There are always many schooling fish at the *Chikuzen,* and a watchful eye may spot a shark or jewfish or sudden schools of pelagic fish, enjoying the sense of adventure of being 70 feet deep out in the open sea.

When the *Chikuzen* first went down in 1981, she was easier to find from the surface, because her hull retained her white paint. Now, the paint has worn off or been covered with corals and algae. Year by year divers have watched the marine life establish itself on the wreck. Little of the life that is seen on the wreck is found in the area surrounding the *Chikuzen.* One wonders how the corals, reef fish, and invertebrates reached this spot so far from established reefs and islands. The building ecosystem on the *Chikuzen* is a reminder of how the open sea carries the tiny larvae of marine creatures.

Humpback Whale Season

January through March in the Virgin Islands provide a constant sense of expectation for those who spend their days on the water, for that is the time of the year when the humpback whales migrate through the area. For the diver it is not unusual in these months to hear the songs of the whales while underwater. Listen carefully and you will the hear the long eerie tones of the humpback singing and perhaps feel chills of delight to know that you swim in the same waters as these giant mammals.

This is a time of year to always keep one eye on the horizon. First a motion attracts your attention, then you see a spout of water that looks like a puff of smoke, a fluke in the air or even a whale breaching. Once the humpbacks surface, it is not unusual to see them again, often several whales, and sometimes with calves. If you are fortunate enough to have them surface near your vessel, you may hear the deep hiss of an exhalation and see the gleaming whiteness on the pectoral fins of these graceful creatures. Sometimes they will swim right under the boat, perhaps turning on their side to stare up at you with one soulful eye.

These winter months, when the playful humpbacks visit the Virgins, are a magical time of year.

The chance to see humpback whales and their calves is a highlight for the visitor to the islands from January through March. (Photo: Jim Scheiner.)

11

Safety

Preparation

Planning for a safe diving trip begins at home. Make sure that your diving equipment has been recently serviced. Pack your certification card and log book. Buy an updated set of dive tables and learn how to use them. If you use a dive computer, install fresh batteries. Bring film, spare batteries and chargers for cameras or underwater flashlights. Be prepared to do a proficiency check of your scuba skills. If you haven't dived for years it makes sense to arrange a refresher course at home or when you reach the islands. Ideally, a well prepared diver is current in first-aid skills and CPR. Check to see if your health insurance covers you in case of a diving accident. If it doesn't, you may wish to purchase supplemental coverage through DAN, available at a nominal cost.

Hazardous Marine Life

For the diver who exercises common sense there are few marine hazards to diving in the British Virgin Islands. If people are injured, it is usually from coral scrapes, fire coral stings, or punctures from the spiny sea urchin. Coral scrapes should be washed with soap and water, and treated with an antiseptic. Stings from fire coral burn for a while, but usually take care of themselves. Sea urchin spines are generally painful for a few days but are quickly absorbed by the body. However, if you are badly injured from any of these, you should have a doctor look at the wound. The bristle worm can also give a burning sting. Be careful if you are picking up an empty conch shell or other object off the bottom, as one could tumble out across your arm.

This lion's mane, accompanied by tiny jacks that seek protection in the tentacles that stream 40 feet behind it, is a marvel to observe but should not be touched. This one was seen above the Chikuzen. (Photo: Linda Sorensen.)

To avoid any injury dive carefully, both for your sake and preservation of the reef. Proper bouyancy control and awareness of your body underwater will minimize abrasion with coral. When entering the water near reef areas, use your mask to look before you step to avoid the obvious hazards. In general, don't touch any marine life with which you are unfamiliar.

In the British Virgin Islands more jellyfish are seen in July and August, when the water is warm, than any other time of year. Large numbers of the beautiful and usually harmless moon jellyfish add a delicate dimension to the blue waters. However, there are a few species that should be avoided. The Portuguese man-of-war, with a purple sail that floats above the water has stinging tentacles that can stream out as far as 60 feet. Although rare in the BVI, they should not be touched if found washed up on the beach or encountered in the water. The lion's mane is similar to the man-of-war but without the sail above water. Box jellies or sea wasps, with tentacles bundled in four clusters, may be found in calm areas and give a bad sting. The small brown jellyfish, with streaming tenacles several feet long are more frequently seen and also to be avoided.

Some individuals are particularly sensitive to stings, which can cause respiratory distress. If you are, talk to your doctor about carrying one of the small bee sting kits and a supply of benedryl. Treatment of jellyfish stings includes the use of household white vinegar, which prevents the nematocysts from firing. Remove tentacles with gloved hands and give aspirin for pain relief. More severe cases may require CPR and immediate medical treatment. As always, prevention is the best remedy. Wear protective clothing such as a wet suit or a Lycra "skin"; wear a mask when you swim and watch where you are going. Nothing can sting you if you don't touch it!

Diving Precautions

Following the basic rules of safe diving are important anywhere you dive. Here are a few additional reminders for your trip to the BVI.

1. Know your own abilities and don't overextend them. If the dive profile sounds strenuous and you aren't a strong swimmer, wait for another chance to dive. Your fellow divers will appreciate your caution.
2. If the currents appear too strong, wait until the conditions change or choose another site.
3. When there is a current, trail a line behind the dive boat to assist any divers who may surface downstream. Descend down a weighted descent line or the anchor line.
4. Topside support is strongly recommended. A qualified operator on the boat can facilitate anyone needing assistance and radio for help if necessary.
5. Have a radio aboard and written emergency numbers and procedures at hand. Portable VHF radios are ideal for small boat diving.
6. Be wary of boat traffic. Don't dive in high traffic areas and listen for the sound of a propeller and engine. Expect that they are not watching out for you.
7. Always fly a dive flag or other marking to clearly indicate you are diving.
8. Follow a current set of dive tables carefully and plan your deepest dives first. Remember precautionary stops at 15 feet, as recommended by the major dive organizations and the suggested surface intervals necessary before flying.

There are numerous well qualified shore-based dive companies and live-aboard charter boats in the BVI ready to take you diving. They provide well equipped boats, with oxygen aboard, and follow well established safety procedures. The personnel are trained in first aid, CPR, and diver rescue and are familiar with the local weather, current, and dive site conditions. Diving with a professional can maximize your vacation time by bringing you safe, comfortable diving with a minimum of hassle. However, if you do decide to dive on your own, realize the responsibility that you need to take for your own safety. Give your diving and emergency procedures careful thought before your trip.

Diver Guidelines for Protecting Reefs*

1. Maintain proper buoyancy control, and avoid over-weighting.
2. Use correct weight belt position to stay horizontal, i.e., raise the belt above your waist to elevate your feet/fins, and move it lower toward your hips to lower them.
3. Use your tank position in the backpack as a balance weight, i.e., raise your backpack on the tank to lower your legs, and lower the backpack on the tank to raise your legs.
4. Watch for buoyancy changes during a dive trip. During the first couple of days, you'll probably breathe a little harder and need a bit more weight than the last few days.
5. Be careful about buoyancy loss at depth; the deeper you go the more your wet suit compresses, and the more buoyancy you lose.
6. Photographers must be extra careful. Cameras and equipment affect buoyancy. Changing f-stops, framing a subject, and maintaining position for a photo often conspire to prohibit the ideal "no-touch" approach on a reef. So, when you must use "holdfasts," choose them intelligently.
7. Avoid full leg kicks when working close to the bottom and when leaving a photo scene. When you inadvertently kick something, stop kicking! Seems obvious, but some divers either semi-panic or are totally oblivious when they bump something.
8. When swimming in strong currents, be extra careful about leg kicks and handholds.
9. Attach dangling gauges, computer consoles, and octopus regulators. They are like miniature wrecking balls to a reef.
10. Never drop boat anchors onto a coral reef.

* Condensed from "Diver Guidelines" by Chris Newbert © Oceanica 1991. Reprinted with permission of Oceanica and Chris Newbert. If you are interested in more information or in helping Oceanica preserve our ocean realm, please write to Oceanica, 342 West Sunset, San Antonio, Texas 78209, USA.

The orange bristle worm lives on the reef flat and in rocky areas under stones or old coral heads. It can grow to 6 inches and the bristles may painfully sting bare hands. (Photo: Jim Scheiner.)

Night Diving

Diving at night is a fascinating way for divers to enjoy the BVI underwater world. Using underwater flashlights, a diver's attention is focused sharply onto the marine life encountered. Because the light is undiluted by the blue filtering effect of the water the colors appear more vibrant than they appear during the day.

Night diving provides the chance to see creatures that hide during the day emerge in search of food. Lobster may be seen marching across the sand and sea urchins move about more actively. Flashlights highlight the brilliant colors and patterns on the body of the sea urchin unappreciated by day.

Blackbar soldierfish and long-spined squirrelfish emerge from their daytime hiding places to feed on the reef and moray eels venture farther from their holes in search of food.

Invertebrates such as this shrimp and anemone entice photographers into macro photography. (Photo: Jim Scheiner.)

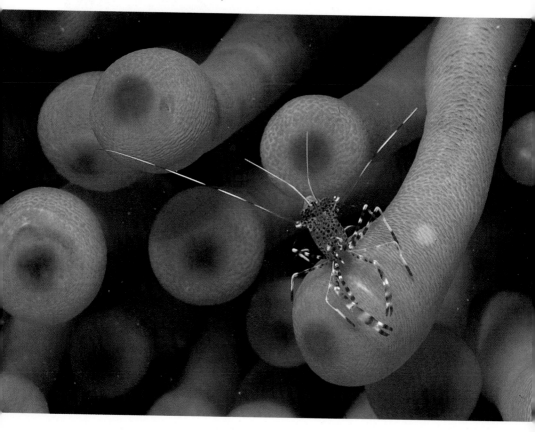

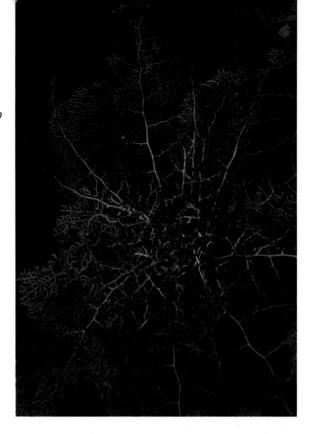

At night the basketstar unfolds hundreds of lacy arms to filter feed food from the water, a captivating sight for the night diver. (Photo: Linda Sorensen.)

Octopus, masters at camouflage during the day, are out on the prowl at night, and if the diver is very lucky he may see an octopus capturing its prey. The octopus saunters over the reef, its body deftly skirting any obstruction. Then, as it targets its prey, the octopus deftly casts its body, like a net, over the unfortunate fish. The fish fights frantically to escape the octopus' grasp, but is gulped into the digestive system. After his meal, the octopus resumes his dance across the reef in search of another tidbit, perhaps changing colors to express his mood about the events of the evening.

Basket starfish are another nighttime marvel. They live tightly entwined in gorgonians, rarely noticed during the day, but at night unfold hundreds of interlacing curling arms to filter food from the water. Tiny shrimp, exactly matching the color of its basketstar host, hide in the entwined arms. The sight of these undulating shapes, perhaps two feet across, adds to the fairyland feel of the nighttime world.

At night it is possible to closely approach fish that would flee in the day. The parrotfish sleeps at night in a protective transparent cocoon of a jelly-like substance secreted through its mouth. They seem comatose, barely moving, and you can closely observe the fish without waking it. Squid, stunned by diver's lights, are also easy and fascinating to examine at night.

Phosphorescent, microscopic organisms, which are invisible during the day, glow in the dark and add to the beauty of a night dive. Watch your buddy's kick stir the water and tiny dots of light burst from the tips of his fins, sparkling like fireflies on a summer night. When there is a full moon and you are diving over a reflective white sand bottom, it is fun to turn off all the lights, let your eyes adjust, and live for a few moments in a magical world of the reef by moonlight. When you move it feels like being on the moon, weightless with the ethereal effect of another world.

When the dive must end and divers emerge from the water into the coolness of a starstudded tropical night, there is a special sense of comraderie that comes only from sharing the wonders of a night dive together.

Emergency Assistance

If you are diving from a boat and have a diving accident that requires emergency assistance, the best thing to do is to call "Mayday" three times on VHF radio Channel 16. Briefly state the name of your boat, your location, and the nature of your emergency. This will clear the channel of other traffic and allows all boats in the area to be alerted to your situation and to offer assistance if possible.

Virgin Islands Radio or Tortola Radio, both monitoring Channel 16, can quickly patch you through to VISAR (Virgin Island Search and Rescue). VISAR can coordinate rescue assistance and place necessary calls to hospitals, helicopter services, or recompression chambers as necessary.

DAN. Whether or not you choose to accept local treatment, our recommendation is that you contact the Divers Alert Network (DAN) in the United States immediately in case of a diving injury. DAN, a membership association of individuals and organizations sharing a common interest in diving safety, operates a **24-hour national hotline, (919) 684-8111** (collect calls are accepted in an emergency). DAN does not directly provide medical care; however, they do provide advice on first aid, evacuation, and hyperbaric treatment of diving-related injuries. For further information, contact DAN, Duke University Medical Center, Box 3823, Durham, NC 27710.

Divers should contact DAN as soon as a diving emergency is suspected. All divers should have comprehensive medical insurance and check to make sure that hyperbaric treatment and air ambulance services are covered internationally.

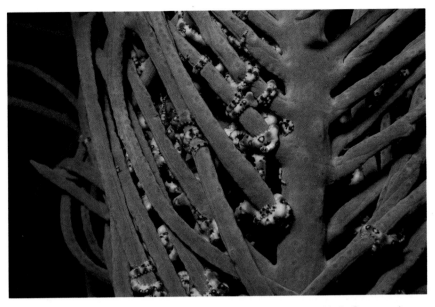

The basketstar lives tightly entwined in a gorgonian by day. (Photo: Linda Sorensen.)

Emergency Numbers

	Radio	Telephone (809)
VISAR Emergency	*	999
VISAR Office		494-4357
Fire and Rescue		999
Virgin Island Radio	Channel l6	776-8282
Tortola Radio	Channel l6	494-4116
U.S. Coast Guard	Channel l6	726-6770
St. Thomas Recompression Chamber		776-2686
St. Thomas Hospital Emergency Room		776-8311 x2221 & x2207
Peebles Hospital, Roadtown		494-3497
Diving Accident Network (DAN) hotline		9l9-684-8111

(*VISAR operates on the radio once contacted through V.I. or Tortola Radio. When calling 999, ask for Fire and Rescue and they will contact a VISAR coordinator.)

Appendix 1: Further Reading

Chaplin, Charles C.G. and Scott, Peter, *Fishwatchers' Guide,* Harrowood Books, Valley Forge, Pennsylvania, 1972.

Humann, Paul, *Reef Fish Identification,* New World Publications, Jacksonville, Florida, 1989.

Jones, A. and Sefton, N., *Marine Life of the Caribbean,* MacMillan Education Limited, London and Basingstoke, 1978.

Marler, George and Luana, *The Royal Mail Steamer* Rhone, Marler Publications Limited, 1978.

Randall, John E., *Caribbean Reef Fishes,* T.F.H. Publications, Inc., Neptune City, New Jersey, revised 1983.

Scott, Simon and Nancy (editors), *The Cruising Guide to the Virgin Islands.* Cruising Guide Publications, Inc., Clearwater, Florida, 1989.

Voss, Gilbert, *Seashore Life of Florida and the Caribbean.* Banyan Books, Inc., Miami, Florida, 1985.

Welcome, published six times per year by Island Publishing Service, Ltd., Roadtown, Tortola, BVI in collaboration with the BVI Tourist Board (800-835-8530) and the Hotel and Commerce Association.

The diver who has experienced the diversity of the diving in the BVI will return home with unforgettable memories. (Photo: Jim Scheiner.)

Appendix 2: Dive Shops and Operations

This information is included as a service to the reader. The author has made every effort to make this list accurate at the time the book was printed. This list does not constitute an endorsement of these operators and dive shops. If operators/owners wish to be considered for future reprints/editions, please contact Pisces Books, P.O. Box 2608, Houston, Texas 77252-2608.

Land-Based Dive Operators

Baskin in the Sun
Prospect Reef, West End, Village Cay
P.O. Box 108
Road Town, Tortola, B.V. I.
800-233-7938
809-494-2858 (Prospect Reef)
809-495-4582 (Soper's Hole)
809-494-4956 (Village Cay)
FAX 809-494-4304

Blue Water Divers
Nanny Cay Resort and Marina
P.O. Box 846
Road Town, Tortola, B.V. I.
809-494-2847
FAX 809-494-0198

Dive BVI
Virgin Gorda Yacht Harbour, Leverick
  Bay, Peter Island
P.O. Box 1040
Virgin Gorda, B.V. I.
1-800-848-7078
809-495-5513 (Virgin Gorda)
809-495-7328 (Leverick Bay)
809-495-9705 (Peter Island)
FAX 809-495-5347

Caribbean Images Tours, Ltd.
Snorkeling Tours
P.O. Box 505
East End, Tortola, B.V. I.
809-494-1147

Kilbrides Underwater Tours
Bitter End, North Sound
P.O. Box 46
Virgin Gorda, B.V. I.
800-932-4286
809-495-9638
FAX 809-495-9638

Underwater Safaris
Moorings Dock, Marina Cay, Cooper Is.
P.O. Box 139
Road Town, Tortola, B.V. I.
800-537-7032
809-494-3235
FAX 809-494-5322

Live-Aboard Dive Boats (BVI-Based)

Cuan Law
105' Trimaran, 20 guests
Trimarine Boat Company
P.O. Box 362
Roadtown, Tortola, B.V.I.
800-648-3393
809-494-2490
FAX 809-494-5774

Encore
53' Trimaran, 8 guests
P.O. Box 3069
Roadtown, Tortola, B.V.I.
809-776-6627

Gypsy Wind
46' Sloop, 2 guests
P.O. Box 3069
Roadtown, Tortola, B.V.I.
809-494-3623

Promenade
65' Trimaran, 10 guests
P.O. Box 3100
Roadtown, Tortola, B.V.I.
809-494-3853

Wanderlust
65' Trimaran, 16 guests
P.O. Box 3069
Roadtown, Tortola, B.V.I.
809-494-3623

Underwater Photographic Specialists

Rainbow Visions Photography
Jim and Odile Scheiner
Rentals, Instruction
Prospect Reef
P.O. Box 680
Road Town, Tortola, B.V.I.
809-494-2749

90

Index